Time: 1970

Cornerstones of Freedom

Kent State

Arlene Erlbach

CHILDREN'S PRESS®
A Division of Grolier Publishing
New York • London • Hong Kong • Sydney
Danbury, Connecticut

Library of Congress Cataloging-in-Publication

Erlbach, Arlene.
  Kent State / Arlene Erlbach.
    p. cm. — (Cornerstones of freedom)
  Includes index.
  ISBN 0-516-20787-3
  1. Kent State University—Riot, May 4, 1970—Juvenile literature. 2.
Student movements—Ohio—Kent—History—20th century—Juvenile
literature. I. Title. II. Series.
LD4191.072E75 1998
378.771'37—dc21
                                                      97-6711
                                                         CIP
                                                          AC

©Children's Press®, a division of Grolier Publishing Co., Inc.
All rights reserved. Published simultaneously in Canada.
Printed in the United States of America.
1 2 3 4 5 6 7 8 9 0 0 7 06 05 04 03 02 01 00 99 98

On May 4, 1970, the unthinkable happened at Kent State University in Kent, Ohio. Members of the Ohio National Guard opened fire on a crowd of college students protesting the Vietnam War and the National Guard's presence on their campus. The shots killed four students and injured nine others. None of the dead students were more than twenty-one years old. One of the injured students was permanently paralyzed. Not all of these students were participating in or even watching the demonstration. Some of them were simply walking to and from class.

In May 1970, Kent State students (two can be seen in the foreground) clashed with members of the Ohio National Guard, leading to tragedy.

"It seemed like a bad dream, but it was real," says Doreen Lazarus, a Kent State student at the time and a reporter for *The Daily Kent Stater,* the campus newspaper.

The tragedy could have taken place on most any college campus during the late 1960s and early 1970s. Major demonstrations at universities such as Columbia, Harvard, and Berkeley had already been major news. Kent State University, however, did not attract large numbers of students likely to begin such demonstrations. The university's student body contained many different types of students, with many different political beliefs.

During demonstrations, students marched and made speeches objecting to issues such as university leadership, unfair treatment of African-Americans, and lack of concern for people in poor

Americans expressed their opinions in demonstrations during the 1960s and 1970s.

countries. They carried signs and recited chants

U.S. soldiers were sent to fight in South Vietnam, a country in southeast Asia.

expressing their views. The most common protests were about the war being fought against North Vietnam, a tiny Asian country 10,000 miles (16,000 kilometers) away from the United States.

President Lyndon
B. Johnson made
the decision to
send large numbers
of U.S. soldiers
to Vietnam.

In 1965, President Lyndon B. Johnson ordered thousands of U.S. soldiers to fight in Vietnam. The United States hoped to prevent the North Vietnamese communist forces from taking over South Vietnam. But as the fighting grew intense, many Americans began to protest against the war. When Richard Nixon became president in 1969, he pledged to bring American soldiers home. In spite of his promises, however, U.S. troops remained, and by 1970, more than one million U.S. soldiers had served in Vietnam. More than fifty thousand of them had died, and hundreds of thousands more had been wounded. It seemed as though there was no end in sight.

At that time, the United States government recruited soldiers by the draft system. When a young man turned eighteen, he registered for the

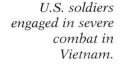

U.S. soldiers
engaged in severe
combat in
Vietnam.

draft. Then they could be selected at random to serve in the army. Once a young man graduated from high school, college, or vocational school, he could be drafted, unless he entered certain fields like teaching or public health. Women entered military service by volunteering. The U.S. government did not draft women.

Many young men did not want to fight a war in a country few people had heard of before 1965. Some men evaded the draft by fleeing to Canada or Sweden, or they joined organizations such as the Peace Corps. Others, called conscientious objectors, declared that their religious or moral beliefs did not allow them to fight in wars.

Young protesters burn their draft cards, which were documents that included their names in the draft.

As the war caused more casualties, many Americans, both young and old, felt that U.S. soldiers should be pulled out of Vietnam. They believed that the war was a drain on the government's money and a waste of life. The country grew divided over the Vietnam War. People opposed to the war were called Doves; those in favor of the war were called Hawks. Many people wore buttons or put bumper stickers on their cars, expressing their views.

In a televised address, President Nixon explains to the American public his plans and reasons for invading Cambodia.

In 1970, the North Vietnamese army crossed into a neighboring country, Cambodia, and constructed military bases. The Cambodians asked the United States for help in driving out the invaders. On Thursday, April 30, President Nixon announced on TV that he was sending U.S. troops into Cambodia. This meant more young men would be drafted. The news sparked loud protests on many college campuses throughout the United States.

On Friday, May 1, a small number of Kent State students marched into the center of Kent and painted antiwar slogans on several buildings. Another quiet protest involving about five hundred students took place on the school's commons, an open area outside Taylor Hall. Students and faculty often used the area to assemble. Some students buried a copy of the U.S. Constitution to symbolize its "murder." These students believed that President Nixon had broken the laws of the Constitution with his latest war strategy. Later that afternoon, Black United Students held a rally that had been planned prior to Nixon's announcement. Another group of students, visiting from Ohio State University in Columbus, discussed recent disorders on their campus.

U.S. tanks and armored personnel carriers move into Cambodia.

That evening the quiet mood of the campus gradually changed. Warm weather brought young people to the strip, an area of bars and shops that were popular hangouts in downtown Kent. Inside the bars, students watched a New York Knicks–Los Angeles Lakers basketball game. People danced and chatted in the streets. The mood was casual, but much talk concerned President Nixon's decision to invade Cambodia.

That night, a disturbing series of incidents occurred. Toward midnight, a police car drove by the strip. Somebody pelted the vehicle with a beer can. Next, someone called for a street gathering. Members of a motorcycle gang built a bonfire in the middle of the street. About four hundred people sang and danced around the fire. Twice as many stood watching on the sidewalks.

The crowd remained peaceful until a man suddenly drove his car through the bonfire. Angry people surrounded the car, smashed its windows, and dented the body. The festive, peaceful atmosphere turned violent. A number of people tossed bottles at store windows, shattering them. Police equipped with riot gear and tear gas ended the evening's chaos. Kent's mayor, LeRoy Satrom, ordered all bars closed and declared that Kent was in a state of civil emergency. He called Ohio's governor, James A. Rhodes, and asked for help to keep order. Rhodes alerted the Ohio National Guard.

The National Guard is a part of the army organized in each state. Members of the guard are called out in state disasters and emergencies. Mayor Satrom placed a curfew on the city of Kent, from 8:00 P.M. to dawn. On Saturday morning, May 2, in spite of the previous night's events, the city and campus

Governor Rhodes reacted to the disorder at Kent State by ordering the National Guard onto the campus.

The curfew kept downtown Kent empty.

remained quiet. Some students walked into downtown Kent and helped merchants clean the mess resulting from Friday's incidents.

Through the late 1960s and 1970s, ROTC buildings became the object of student anger on many campuses. This ROTC building burns at the University of Ohio in Akron.

Other students, however, were still angry, and rumors flew about what might happen next. Some said that demonstrators might try to burn down the Army Reserve Officers Training Corps (ROTC) barracks. In this building, students trained to become military officers. During the Vietnam War years, the ROTC drew the anger of students on many college campuses. Its presence symbolized the military and the war. On some campuses, students had already destroyed the campus ROTC building.

In addition to rumors about the ROTC, some people had heard that Students for a Democratic Society (SDS) had come to the campus. This group of students promoted antiwar protests at college campuses around the country. The previous spring, the SDS had threatened to close Kent State down through demonstrations. University officials worried that the SDS might try again.

As the unrest grew, Kent State University president Robert I. White was away at a conference in Iowa. University vice president Robert Matson, who was in charge, organized activities to keep students occupied on campus. He hired a rock band for a dance to keep students away from town and under the curfew. Few students attended.

University vice president Robert Matson tried to keep the campus calm.

At about 6:00 P.M., May 2, approximately fifty students began protesting on the school commons. In less than two hours the crowd grew to more than six hundred students. Led by a small group, the crowd marched through dormitories, attracting more students.

Shortly after 8:00 P.M., an angry crowd of more than one thousand people reached the ROTC building. Someone tossed a rock at the building. Another unfurled an American flag, ripped it, and burned it. A few others managed to set the building on fire. Moments later, a fire truck arrived, but some demonstrators would not allow firefighters to put out the fire. They grabbed the firehose nozzle, stopping the firefighters from extinguishing the blaze. When firefighters set up a second hose, protesters attacked with knives, ice picks, and a machete. The firefighters, concerned for their own safety, left the scene. Shortly afterward, nine hundred members of the National Guard moved into the university and stationed themselves all over the campus.

The guard warned students to return to their dorms. Some students refused. Others threw rocks at the guard members. The guardsmen used tear gas and rifles with fixed bayonets to bring the situation under control.

Guardsmen move onto the Kent State campus.

On Sunday morning, helicopters hovered over the campus. The Guard stood ready with tear gas and M-1 rifles equipped with bayonets, in case of more unrest. That morning, Governor Rhodes arrived to view the situation. The county prosecutor, Ronald Kane, suggested that the governor close down the university to avoid further trouble. The governor refused. He believed that such a strategy would give in to SDS, or whoever was behind the recent disruption.

Meetings took place with the governor, student body president Frank Frisina, Vice President Robert Matson, and university officials. The meetings, however, resulted in conflicting views of the situation by both the students and the authorities. Students were not sure who was in charge of the campus—the National Guard, the Ohio state government, or the university.

On Sunday afternoon, Frisina and Matson issued a flyer warning students not to take part in activities that could lead to confrontations with the guard. The flyer contained the following information:

1) All forms of outdoor demonstration were prohibited.
2) The guard was empowered to make arrests.
3) A curfew from 8:00 P.M. to 6:00 A.M. in the city and to 1:00 A.M. on campus was in effect.

The flyer was not seen by all students. Those living off campus did not receive the flyer. Some students living in dormitories did not check their mailboxes. It was not clear whether or not rallies were allowed, and no one seemed to know the exact curfew time. The campus became full of confusion.

The campus remained calm most of Sunday and became a magnet for sightseers. Some picnicked on the commons with their families. Others had their pictures taken with the guard. Some students even acted friendly towards the guardsmen. Allison Krause, one of the students who would later be slain, is said to have noticed a flower in the muzzle of one soldier's rifle and discussed the flower with the guardsman. Moments later, an officer ordered the young man to remove the flower. "Flowers are better than

Guardsmen order the crowd to disperse.

bullets," Allison retorted. This phrase would later be etched on her gravestone.

About 9:00 P.M. Sunday evening, students held a peaceful rally on the commons. Concerned that the gathering could turn violent, a guard officer ordered the crowd to disperse, or break apart and leave. When many of the demonstrators refused to do so, guardsmen fired tear gas. A mob of demonstrators marched toward East Main and Lincoln Streets, near the entrance of the university, and blocked traffic. One of the leaders of the march told students that they would be able to speak to President White and Mayor Satrom about the curfew, but nobody arrived to speak with them. Again, the guardsmen attempted to disperse the crowd. An officer announced that the 1:00 A.M. curfew had been moved back to 11:00 P.M.

The crowd now became hostile and shouted taunts at the guardsmen. Others threw rocks. For about a half-hour, guardsmen chased those who refused to go back into the dorms. Both guardsmen and demonstrators were injured in the confusion, and anger between the two groups replaced the relaxed mood from the previous day.

Some daring students threw tear gas canisters back toward the guard.

While many students were aware that rallies had been banned, others knew nothing about the prohibition. Students who lived at home returned to class on Monday morning. They were unaware about the curfew and the rules against assembly. Even without a rally, the commons would be crowded at noon. Many students would cross this area to get to classes, the library, or lunch. On a lovely spring day, like May 4, students might stop in groups to enjoy the sun or chat.

At about noon, more than two thousand students stood on the commons. Some planned to take part in the rally. Others were there just to observe. Some were simply walking across the commons. A university patrolman, driven in a jeep occupied by three guardsmen, ordered the crowd to disperse. The students responded by throwing rocks and cursing at them. Guardsmen fired tear gas, but wind blew the tear gas back. Many students now left the commons, although some remained, taunting the guard with rocks and threats.

Tear gas canisters explode among the crowd.

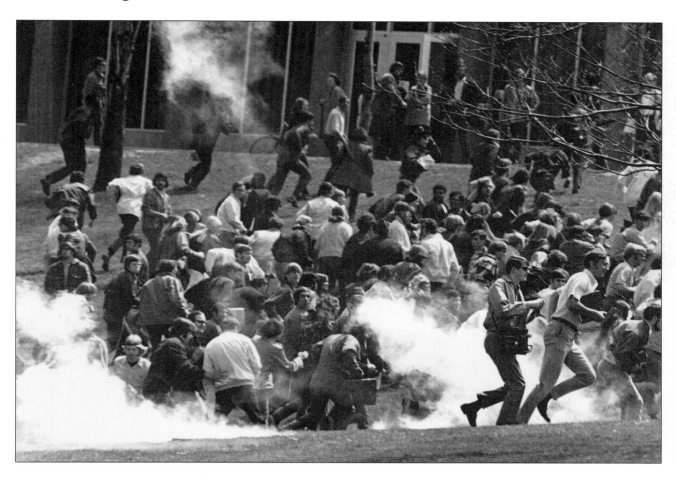

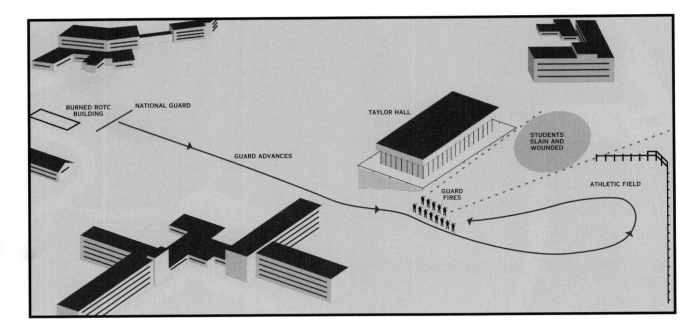

BURNED ROTC
BUILDING

NATIONAL GUARD

TAYLOR HALL

STUDENTS
SLAIN AND
WOUNDED

GUARD ADVANCES

ATHLETIC FIELD

GUARD
FIRES

*This map shows
the path the
guard took before
stopping and firing.*

About one hundred guardsmen now formed a line and started walking across the commons toward the demonstrators. The students retreated back up a hill and around Taylor Hall. The guard followed them, marching into an empty athletic field on the other side. Suddenly, the guard found themselves blocked by fences bordering the field. There was nothing for them to do but retreat. Daring students continued to harass them, throwing rocks and shouting insults.

The guardsmen moved back up the hill toward Taylor Hall, followed by the taunting demonstrators. Moments later, about twenty-eight guardsmen turned around and leveled their rifles at the students, most of whom were

less than 100 yards (91 meters) away. Suddenly, the noisy buzz of the crowd was shattered by the sound of gunshots. The guardsmen fired a volley of about sixty-five shots for approximately thirteen seconds. Some of the guardsmen aimed their rifles into the air, but others fired directly into the crowd.

The guard, formed in a line in the middle of the photograph, starts moving toward the students in the foreground.

William Schroeder, Allison Krause, Jeffrey Miller, and Sandra Lee Scheuer, the four young people killed on May 4, 1970.

At first, some of the students did not believe that the guardsmen had used live ammunition. Most demonstrators thought the guns held blanks. Other students realized what was happening and ran screaming. The shots killed Allison Krause, William Schroeder, Sandra Lee Scheuer, and Jeffrey Miller almost instantly, and wounded nine others.

This photograph shows the guard just seconds after they finished shooting. Several students help a wounded man on the sidewalk.

The incident frightened and shocked the students. Some students tried to administer first aid to the wounded. But moments later, feelings of disbelief turned to anger. A group of more than two hundred demonstrators gathered on a nearby slope. They refused to leave until convinced by faculty members that they must move. That afternoon, President White ordered the university closed.

Hours after the shooting, a group of students and the National Guard stand tensely only a few hundred feet apart. The remains of the burned ROTC building are in the foreground.

23

ALLISON KRAUSE

In the coming days, all students, faculty, and staff had to leave. Kent State students finished their coursework for the quarter in makeshift classrooms or by mail. The tragedy sent shockwaves through the nation and around the world. More than two hundred college campuses across the nation shut down temporarily because of student strikes. The university received dozens of letters from high school students, and one from Jonathan Pannor, a nine-year-old boy, living in California. "The tragedy really affected me," said Jonathan, recalling the incident. "The United States' involvement with Vietnam had been happening all my life. Now, killing was happening right here to students, bigger than me, on what appeared to be a giant playground."

Many people sympathized with the students and their families. Others thought the students were at fault and more should have been shot. Some guardsmen claimed their lives had been threatened. The questions of who really was at fault, and who should be prosecuted needed to be answered.

One of the earliest investigations into the incident, done by the President's Commission on Campus Unrest, concluded that the shootings were unnecessary and inexcusable. So did a letter from the U.S. Justice Department, urging that charges be brought against the guardsmen. In October 1970, however, a state grand jury found the guardsmen innocent of any crime. The jury charged twenty-four students, other young people, and a Kent State professor with arson, inciting a riot, and interfering with a fireman. About a year later, the charges were dropped. It seemed that the tragic incident of May 4, 1970, might fade into history and be forgotten. But it did not.

Many people, including Allison Krause's parents, demanded justice for the shootings.

In 1973, due to public and media pressure, the Justice Department reopened the criminal case. A federal grand jury ruled that eight guardsmen should stand trial for shooting the students. But the judge, Frank Battisti, dismissed the charges before the case went to trial. He ruled that the prosecutors had failed to prove the case beyond a reasonable doubt.

In May 1975, five years after the tragedy, a civil trial was finally held. After three months of testimony, the jury ruled in favor of the National Guard. None of the plaintiffs could receive damages.

Two years later, an appeals court overturned the 1975 civil court decision on the basis that the judge had mishandled a threat to a juror. A retrial began in 1978. The victims settled out of court

Members of the National Guard who were tried for the shootings.

in 1979 for $675,000, paid by the state of Ohio. The court split the money thirteen ways, among the parents of the deceased students and each of the wounded students.

Dean Kahler, who was permanently paralyzed, received half of the money. Fifteen thousand dollars went to each of the parents of the slain children to compensate for their loss. The remainder of the money was divided among the rest of the students, depending on the severity of their injuries.

As part of the out-of-court settlement, twenty-eight guardsmen, without stating guilt or innocence, signed a short statement that in part read:

"We deeply regret those events and are profoundly saddened by the deaths of four students and the wounding of nine others which resulted. We hope that the agreement to end this litigation will help to assuage the tragic memories regarding the sad day."

Dean Kahler (shown here in 1990), was paralyzed below his waist by the shootings.

Twenty years after the tragedy, a new generation of Kent State students remembered.

The university has not forgotten the tragedy. In May 1984, university president Michael Schwartz and the Kent State University Board of Trustees decided to build a memorial to commemorate the incident. On January 25, 1989, ground was broken for a memorial site.

On May 4, 1990, twenty years after the incident, a formal ceremony was held to dedicate the memorial. Then-governor of Ohio, Richard Celeste, apologized to the victims, their families and friends, and the university on behalf of the state. The memorial rests on a 2.5 acre site overlooking the commons where the incident

The Kent State Memorial is the low structure in the middle of this photograph. The flowers in the foreground are a memorial to the United States servicemen who lost their lives in Vietnam.

occurred. It contains a granite plaza and four granite disks leading to a wooded area. Engraved on a plaque north of the memorial are the names of the students killed and injured. Every spring, 58,175 daffodils bloom to remember the American servicemen and servicewomen who lost their lives in Vietnam.

At the plaza's threshold on three reflective stones are inscribed the words "Inquire, Learn, Reflect." These words are designed to encourage visitors to inquire about the event, to learn about it, and to reflect on how people's differences can be peacefully resolved.

This photograph, showing a young girl's horrified reaction to the death of another student, won a Pulitzer Prize and became famous through-out the world.

GLOSSARY

accuse – to blame

defendants

civil suit – lawsuit that tries to determine if someone must pay money for injuring someone else

defendant – party or parties who answer the claims in a legal action

demonstration – an outward display about an issue

draft – recruitment of people to join the military by legal force

Grand Jury – legal group of citizens that decides whether a case should go to trial

National Guard – military reserve forces organized by state

protest

Peace Corps – organization that sends volunteers to help people in foreign countries

plaintiff – person who files a lawsuit to seek a remedy for injuries or rights

protest – to disagree

ROTC – stands for Reserve Officers Training Corps, a program that trains officers for the military

TIMELINE

1965
Lyndon Johnson orders large numbers of U.S. soldiers to Vietnam

Richard Nixon elected president **1968**

1970

April 30: Nixon announces sending troops into Cambodia

May 1: Violent protests erupt in downtown Kent

May 2: ROTC building burned; the National Guard arrives in Kent

May 3: Confrontation between demonstrators and guardsmen

May 4: Guardsmen fire on students, killing four and wounding nine

October: The President's Commission on Campus Unrest concludes the shootings were unnecessary; a state grand jury finds the guardsmen not guilty and finds twenty-four students and a professor guilty of various charges

1973 The Justice Department reopens the criminal case

1974 ⎫
1975 ⎭ Civil trials by parents of dead students and injured students are held

1978 ⎫
1979 ⎭ A new civil trial is held; parents and victims settle out of court

1984 University officials decide to build a memorial in memory of the incident

1990 The memorial is dedicated

DEDICATION

In memory of Allison Krause, Jeffrey Miller, Sandra Scheuer, and William Schroeder.

Respectfully acknowledged: Alan Canfora, John Cleary, Thomas Grace, Dean Kahler, Joseph Lewis, Donald McKenzie, James Russell, Robert Stamps, and Douglas Wrentmore.

The author would like to thank the following people for their time and help in making this project possible: Dr. James Banks, Ms. Nancy Birk, Ms. Margaret Garmon, Mr. James Harris, Mr. Dean Kahler, Ms. Doreen Lazarus, Dr. Jerry M. Lewis, Mr. Jonathan Pannor, and Ms. Paula Slimak.

INDEX (*Boldface* page numbers indicate illustrations.)

PHOTO CREDITS

Photographs ©: AP/Wide World Photos: 11 bottom, 12, 14, 22 bottom, 23, 24, 31 top left; Archive Photos: 7; Consolidated News/Archive Photos: 6 top, 31 top right; Gamma-Liaison: 1 (Michael Abramson); The Image Works: 28 top (Fossett), 31 bottom (J. Fossett); John Paul Filo: cover, 3, 21, 29; Kent State University Archives, University News and Information: 28 bottom; The Nixon Project, National Archives: 8; Tom Myers: 4, 30 bottom; U.S. Air Force: 6 bottom; UPI/Corbis-Bettmann: 2, 9, 11 top inset, 13, 15, 17, 18, 19, 22 top, 25, 26, 27, 30 top.

ABOUT THE AUTHOR

Arlene Erlbach has written more than thirty books. Her first book, *Does Your Nose Get in the Way, Too?*, won a Romance Writer's of America RITA for best young adult novel of the year. In addition to being an author, Arlene is a special education teacher at the William P. Gray school in Chicago. She is also in charge of the school's young author program.

Arlene was a student at Kent State when the shooting occurred. She hopes that her book will explain the incident to young people and inspire them to think about ways people can peacefully resolve their differences.

Arlene lives in Morton Grove, Illinois with her husband, her teenage son, a collie, and two cats.